Investing!

Blunt and to the Point

Sponsored by

Helping the world A.I.M for success!

Thank you to the following individuals.

You provided me motivation.

You provided me the confidence.

This book is a reality because of you

I could not have done it without you.

Thank You!

Aaron Wahnish

Alfred Escobari

Alina Sahakian

Anthony Head

Artin Sahakian

Charlie Miott

Christos Vodos

Donna Facciola

Daquan Page

Frank DeLeon

Gabriella Jibaja

Gina Anton

Josephine Wiles

Khalida Rafiqi

Kush Jenkins

Lacey Sherman

Leila McDowell

Lewis Anton

Mani Fierro

Mark Nober

Mayo Welch

Michael Brazie

Nanette Wahnish

Roya Makki

Shawn Miles

Taylor McIntosh

Tony Head

Tiffney Laing

Weldon Thompson

Zahara Hassan

Our Partner Projects

Motivational Videos for Success

YouTube.com/LaunchMySuccess

A.I. Textbooks, LLC
Find the best price online for Textbooks

Awesome Ideas

AwesomeTextbooks.com

My name is Joshua Anton, and I am a student investor. Born in New York City, where we tell it like it is, I am going to be honest. Anyone can invest.

Currently, I attend the University of Virginia, McIntire School of Commerce. Before becoming a student at UVA, I went to Northern Virginia Community College for three years. Before that, I was a student in special education. I am not rich. In fact, I make less than $20,000 a year. Yet I make a little bit of extra money each month from investing. Any student can invest.

Adversity is a significant part of my life. From having been kicked out of the house as a senior in high school to working thirty hours a week pushing carts at the local grocery store to figuring out how to pay for my living expenses, it was hard to save up enough money to invest. It was even harder to say to myself, "I am going to risk $4,000 and invest in the stock market."

I am not going to lie to you; I was scared, and I knew it was risky. Four thousand dollars is a lot of money to most people. I gained money in the beginning, and I lost some money, too. However, once I got the hang of it, it was kind of cool to make an extra $300 a month. I could use the money to pay my phone bill or to go out to eat a few more times a week. That's one benefit of investing. I am not super rich because I invest, but I do like having a little bit of extra cash. All calculated risks can have great rewards. To be blunt, I am confident that if I could invest, you can too.

Why You Should Invest

You don't have to be an expert to invest. All you have to do is take a chance and learn a new skill. My story may remind you of yourself or of someone you may know. You may know a student or someone who works in a grocery store. Think about how many people are mentally or physically exhausted from their jobs. Consider the number of people who just want to have an extra day every now and then to spend some quality time with their family or their friends. Do you know students who work thirty hours a week to pay for school? Most people just want a way out, a little bit more money, or a little bit more time. Investing grants that. You may not be rich when you finish investing, but you will have a little bit more money and plenty of time to spend with your family and friends.

For instance, Warren Buffet, one of the greatest investors of our time, started from humble beginnings. He started just like us. He was just a regular boy throwing newspapers at people's doors in the morning. Then he saved up a bit of money and tried to invest. He definitely failed a few times and made some bad investments. However, we all make mistakes. What if he had chosen not to risk his small newspaper salary at the time? What if he had chosen to play it safe? If he chose not to take the risk, would we know the name Warren Buffet today?

Anyone Can Invest

Look, there are probably people reading this who are somewhat squeamish about investing. Let's be frank: Anyone can invest.

Yes, you may be scared that you will lose your money, but we are scared about a lot of things. What overcomes our fear? Doing it. Taking a chance.

You may be worried because you don't have any idea about how to invest. Let me ask you. How do you gain knowledge? You ask questions, you find more information, and then you go do it.

You may not understand how business works whatsoever, and everything from business to finance may confuse you. Don't worry. Business is common sense. It is similar to predicting how someone will react to an event. The same applies to a company on the stock market.

You may have not tried to invest because you believe you are not good at math. First, accounting and calculus are not anyone's best friends. You don't have to be a financial genius to invest. You need to know basic investing knowledge, you need be able to think creatively, and you just need to try it.

There are probably many other reasons you have not invested, but the main point is that anyone can learn to invest. All anyone needs to do is make a choice, ask questions, seek knowledge, and go do it. How do you think I went from the verge of homelessness to a UVA student? I asked questions, I made a choice to set my sights high, I sought out knowledge, and I went out and applied to the school. Investing is very similar.

To become an investor is risky and rewarding. You will earn money on the stock market. You will lose money on the stock market. You will learn how to think critically, reflect on your mistakes, and do better. You will fail, and you will succeed. This is the journey of an investor. Investing is not a gamble on which stock will do better. It is an art and a science. It is the ability to make an educated guess on how, why, and when a stock will do well.

Why invest? This is simple: More time, more money. The underlying reasons behind those results are irrelevant. Some people may want more time for their families; some may want secondary income. Some may invest so they can show future employers such as bankers that they have experience. Investing is taking a chance, but the reason that most people invest is to make more money and to have more time.

This book is not going to teach you how to become an expert investor overnight. Investing on an expert level takes time and experience. This book will give you the tools and concepts you will need to learn about investing. It provides the resources you need to help you consider why you should invest.

The goal of this book is to provide a point and a place to obtain more information. An eighty-page book won't tell you all the aspects of investing and how to do it. Honestly, neither would a 2,000-page book on investing. You learn through experience.

Provide a point and a place to go: What if your dream were to become an artist? What if you were given the supplies and the knowledge of how to research and practice and where to find more information? What if all of this could make your dream to become an artist a reality? Would you become an artist?

Provide a point and a place to go: What if this book gave you the resources to become an investor within a few months? What if you were given the tools to start investing, the main points, a place to obtain more information, and the roadmap of resources to ask for help when you needed it? Would you take the chance and become an investor?

Mary Oliver, an American author once said, "What are you doing with that crazy precious life of yours?" I now will ask something similar: What are you doing with it? Why aren't you investing? Why might you be scared of investing and potentially losing your money? Are you afraid to make a mistake? Are you afraid you may fail?

If you don't take a chance and try to invest, you will never become an investor. You will only be someone who knows a lot from reading and talking but who never applies this investment knowledge. How many people do you know who may have the knowledge to invest but don't? How many of these people don't invest because they are scared or uncomfortable with the risk?

What if you lost $1,500 of a $4,000 portfolio, but you learned a valuable lesson you will never repeat as long as you are an investor. Is this not a valuable way to spend $1,500? In fact, some of us may spend much more on alcohol, videos, cigarettes, fast food, clubbing, or other wasteful things in one to three months! Sometimes lessons, such as divorces or foreclosures, could cost tens of thousands of dollars. Losing $1,500 sounds like a bargain, doesn't it? It's about perspective. You have to risk something to gain something. Yes, when you invest, you may lose money, but more often than not, you will gain money. You have to try to do it to make that extra few hundred a month.

There are three questions I ask you as you read this book. What risks are you willing to take for more time and more money? If you were given the tools and the knowledge to invest, would you be ready to take a chance and use these tools to become an investor? What do you plan to do with that crazy precious life of yours?

Chap 1: *Start an Investment Account*

To Draw
You Need Crayons

To Invest
You Need An
Investment Account

What Makes an Investment Agency Awesome?

Customer Service

Fees

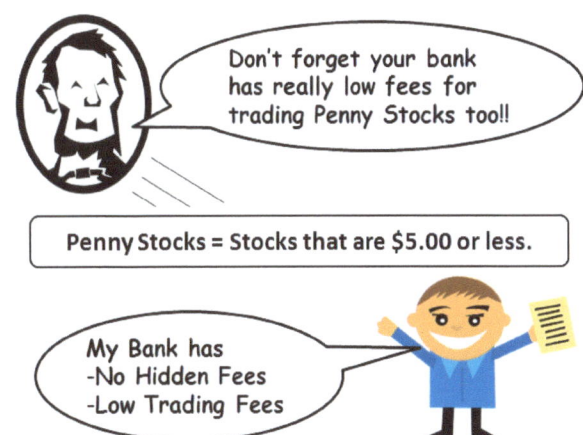

Don't forget your bank has really low fees for trading Penny Stocks too!!

Penny Stocks = Stocks that are $5.00 or less.

My Bank has
-No Hidden Fees
-Low Trading Fees

Minimum Starting Balance

E*TRADE requires me to have a minimum balance

But, my bank said I don't need a minimum balance!

Wow!!

How good is the Trading Platform?

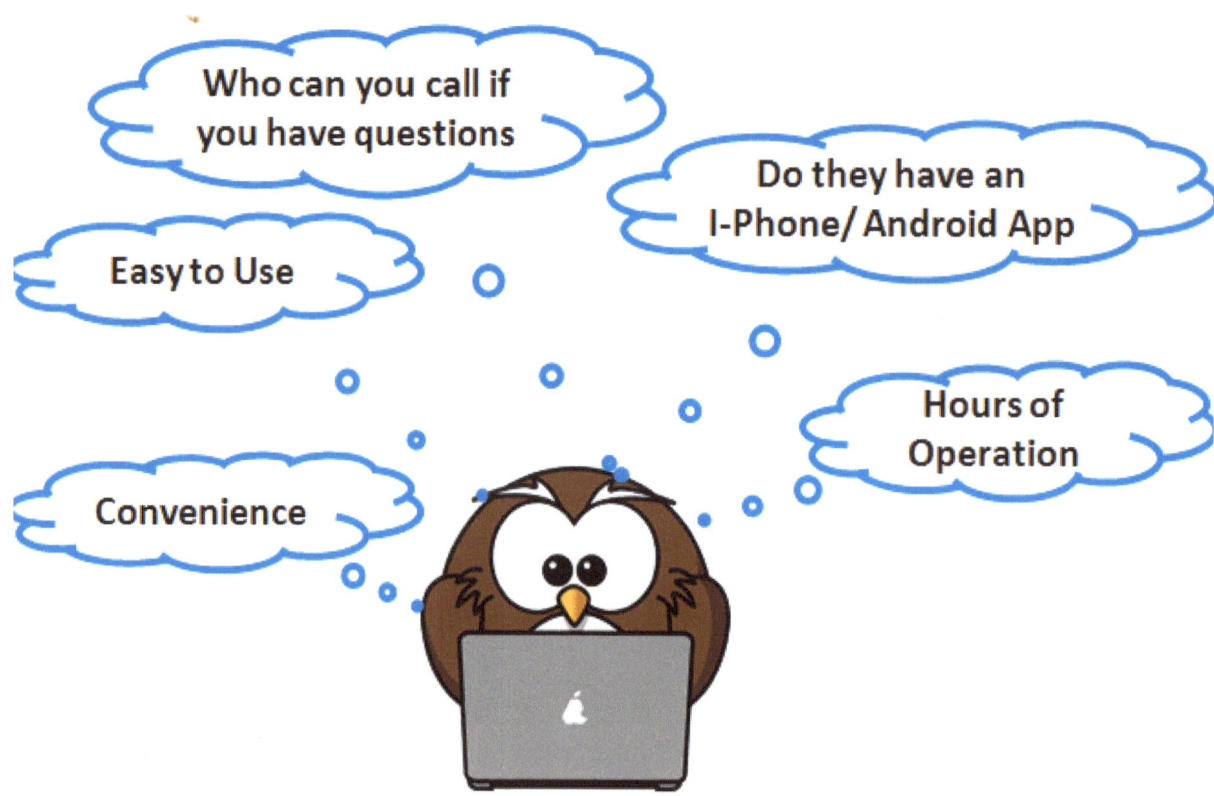

How Easy is it to Transfer Money from Your Bank Account to Your Investment Account?

Investment Agencies

Brick and Mortar Banks	Online Investment Services
USAA: Investment Banking Minimal Investment: None www.usaa.com	**Scott Trade** Minimal Investment: Yes www.scottrade.com
PNC Bank Minimal Investment: None www.pnc.com	**eTrade** Minimal Investment: Yes www.etrade.com
SunTrust Minimal Investment: None www.suntrust.com	**Fidelity** Minimal Investment: Yes www.fidelity.com
TD - Ameritrade Minimal Investment: None www.tdbank.com	

You can also trade IRAs, Mutual Funds, and Bonds

with these investment brokers.

But we are going to focus in our book specifically on trading stocks for capital gain. (Profit)

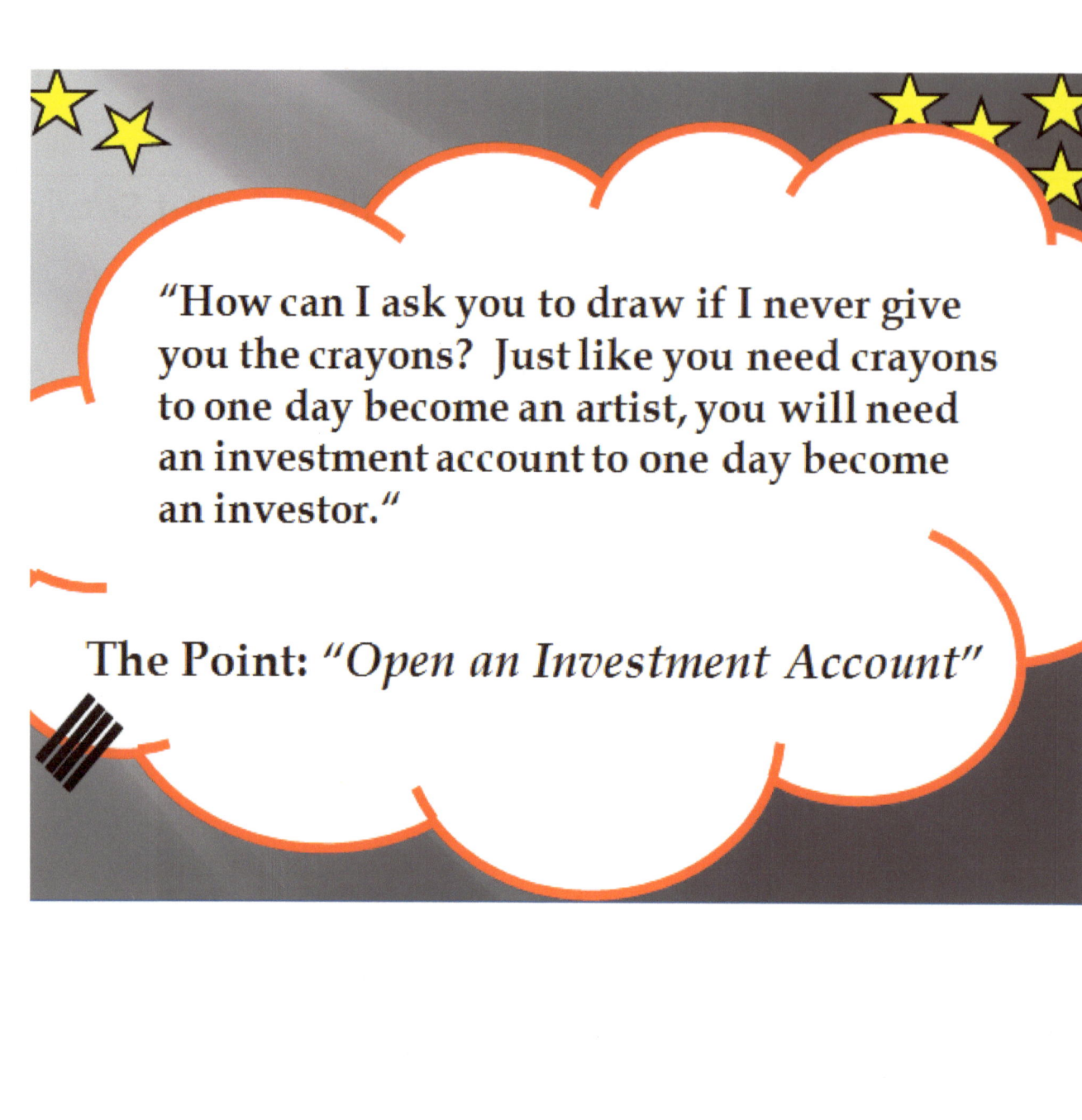

Resources

- ☑ *Investment Account*
- ☐ $1,500 - $3,000 in savings to start investing
- ☐ Websites to Practice Investing
- ☐ Websites to Research Investing

Knowledge

- ☐ Do I understand generally how the stock market works?
- ☐ Do I know how to read a stock graph?
- ☐ Do I know the basics on how and why stock prices change?

Questions for Yourself

- ☐ Am I investing with money that is not essential for my survival, such as rent, food, electricity, car payment?
- ☐ Do I know whom to go to if I have any questions?
- ☐ Am I aware that I could lose money when I invest?
- ☐ Am I comfortable knowing that I may make mistakes when I invest and that these mistakes will show me what not to do and help build my experience as an investor?
- ☐ Do I know how to purchase and sell stocks through my investment account?

Critical Thinking

- ☐ Do I know how to predict whether or not a company will go bankrupt?
- ☐ Do I know how to research a company and make my own conclusions about whether or not I should invest?
- ☐ Do I know how to determine why a stock price will change (increase or decrease?)

Chap 2: *Start Saving*

A Few Tips to
Start Saving Today

By... You may save...

By **Carpooling** to work once a week: → You may save *$50.00* a month

By making **Coffee** at home → You may save *$40.00* a month

By **Smoking 2 Less** cigarettes a day → You may save *$40.00* a month

By reviewing your current **Phone Plan** → You may save *$20.00* a month

By buying **Water/Sodas** in 12 packs rather than in vending machines → You may save *$20.00* a month

By bringing **Lunch from Home** to work rather than eating out →You may save *$100.00* a month

By using **Hulu and YouTube** rather than cable → You may save *$25.00* a month

By turning off the **Lights and Unplugging Unused Devices** at home → You may save *$80.00* a Month

By **Eating at Home** and not going out to eat → You may save *$150.00* a month

By drinking two less **Alcoholic Drinks** a week → You may save *$40.00* a month

By buying **Generic** items rather than name brand items → You may save *$50.00* a month

By getting rid of the **Landline Phone** in place of a mobile phone → You may save *$40.00* a month

By buying items like paper towels, soap, etc. in **Bulk** → You may save *$40.00* a month

By **Saving** 5% - 10% of one's paycheck → *You will have money when you need it*

By Following These Directions → Some will save over $500.00 a Month

How much will you save?

The Art of Savings

1. *Have a Goal!* What are you saving for? How much for you need?

2. Save 5% - 10% of each paycheck. *Extra money is never a bad thing.*

3. Never go to the grocery store or restaurant extremely hungry. *When you are hungry you buy more.*

4. *Reward yourself*, when you hit your savings goal. Something that says, "I'm awesome I hit my savings goal!"

5. Before buying something, "Ask yourself, *Do you really need it*" it will stop you from buying stuff you don't need

6. For bigger purchases such as a T.V., Textbooks for school, Furniture, even Cars, there are lot of resources out there that you don't have to go out and spend a lot of money on these items, where you can save a lot of money
    a. Craigslist (Furniture, T.V's, Cars, and of course cardboard boxes)
    b. www.awesometextbooks.com (Textbooks)
    c. Your friends (All of the above)
    d. Compare Prices on big purchases on E-Bay and Amazon.

Basically, get addicted to savings.

*I learned this lesson when I saw my tax return and realized I wasted $9,000 in a year as a 16 year old

Author's Note:

You can start investing with just $200.00. But there is a better way you can invest.

My advice is to save $2,000 before you invest for two reasons.

1. **Fees: The less you invest, the more your fees affect your profit.**
2. **Diversification:** Investing in 2–3 stocks allows you to lose money on one company but earn money on the other—limiting your losses and risk.

*Fees are the cost to make a trade (buy or sell stocks) set by your investment broker. The fee varies from as little as $6 to as much as $12.00 per trade.

Figure 2.1

You invest a certain amount of money *(outlined in blue)*
You make a 10% profit *(outlined in green)*
How fees affect the profit you receive *(outlined in red)*

The fees to buy and sell your stocks are **$20.00**

Your Investment	Your Profit	Your Profit - After Fees
$200	$20	0
$400	$40	$20
$600	$60	$40
$800	$80	$60
$1,000	$100	$80

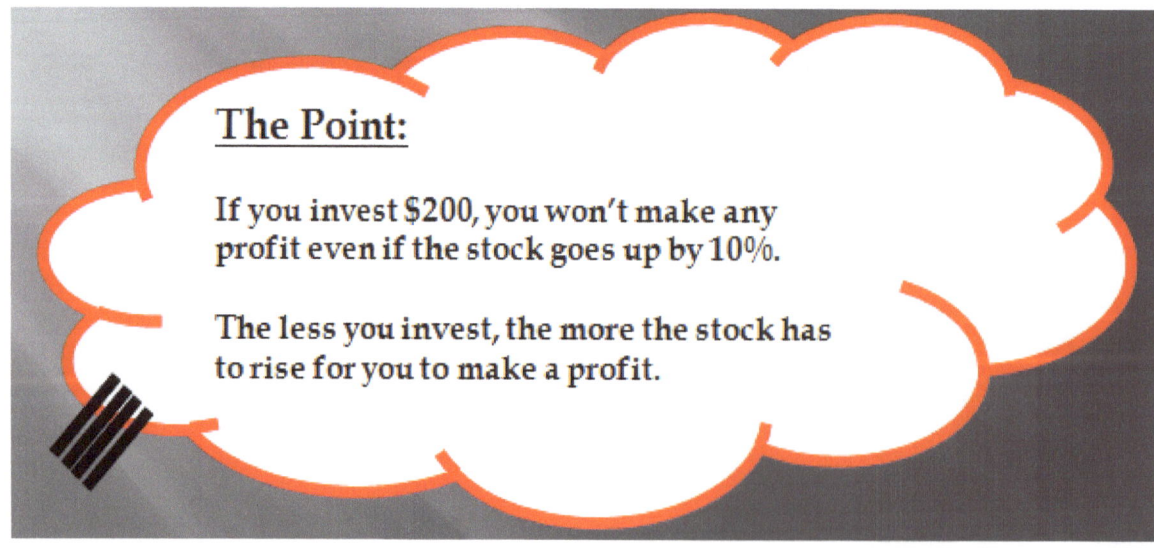

The Point:

If you invest $200, you won't make any profit even if the stock goes up by 10%.

The less you invest, the more the stock has to rise for you to make a profit.

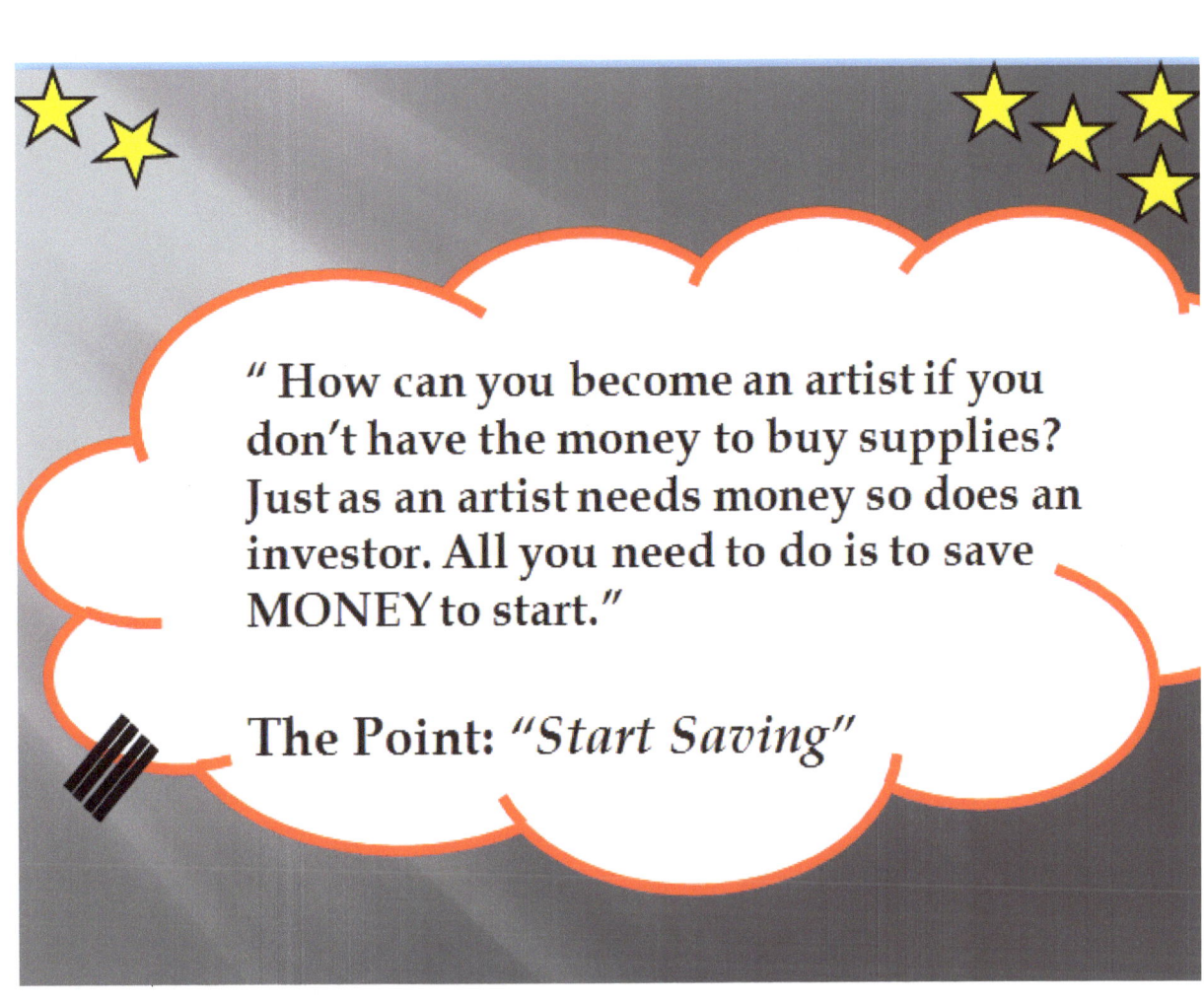

" How can you become an artist if you don't have the money to buy supplies? Just as an artist needs money so does an investor. All you need to do is to save MONEY to start."

The Point: *"Start Saving"*

Congratulations!! _You are just a little bit closer to becoming an investor._

**The Points that are** Bolded in RED **are the points we have covered in this chapter!**

**Before you move on to the next chapter, you should understand why these concepts are essential in order for you to become an investor. Keep on reading! You are doing great!**

Resources

- ☑ **Investment Account**
- ☑ *$1,500 - $3,000 in savings to start investing*
- ☐ Websites to Practice Investing
- ☐ Websites to Research Investing

Knowledge

- ☐ Do I understand generally how the stock market works?
- ☐ Do I know how to read a stock graph?
- ☐ Do I know the basics on how and why stock prices change?

Questions for Yourself

- ☑ *Am I investing with money that is not essential for my survival, such as rent, food, electricity, car payment?*
- ☐ Do I know whom to go to if I have any questions?
- ☐ Am I aware that I could lose money when I invest?
- ☐ Am I comfortable knowing that I may make mistakes when I invest and that these mistakes will show me what not to do and help build my experience as an investor?
- ☐ Do I know how to purchase and sell stocks through my investment account?

Critical Thinking

- ☐ Do I know how to predict whether or not a company will go bankrupt?
- ☐ Do I know how to research a company and make my own conclusions about whether or not I should invest?
- ☐ Do I know how to determine why a stock price will change (increase or decrease?)

Chap 3: *Practice Investing*

Practice Investing

"It won't make you perfect, but you will learn a lot."

Start a Virtual Investment Account

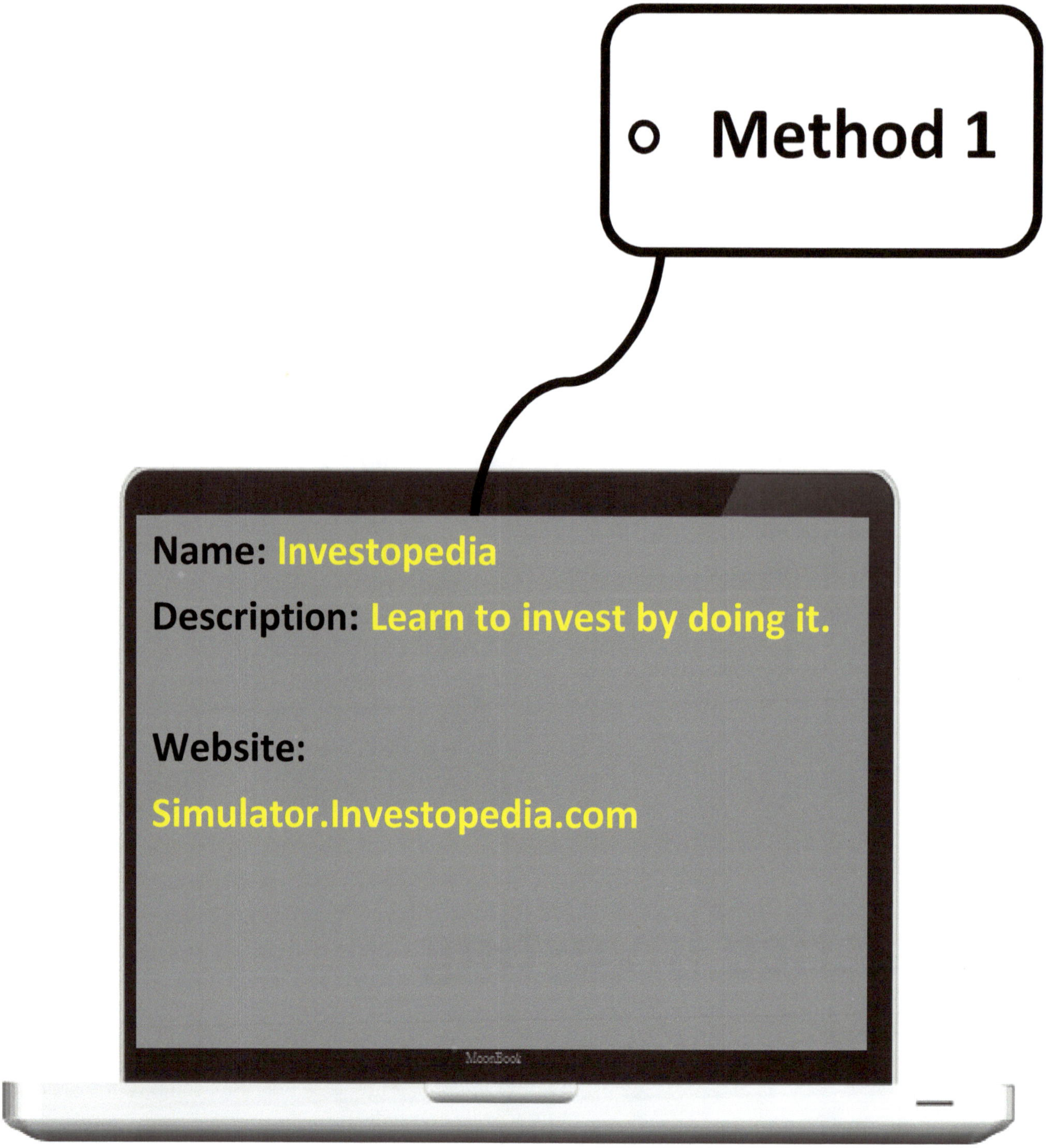
Method 1
Name: Investopedia
Description: Learn to invest by doing it.
Website:
Simulator.Investopedia.com

Two-Month Tracking Activity

This activity will help you practice trading on the stock market.

Please follow the following steps:

1. **Print out the sheet on the next page (or copy it, if you have a hard copy of my book).**
2. **Pick four or five stocks you would invest in and fill out the details on the sheet below.**
3. **Every Friday, document the following:**
    - Changes in the stock (specifically its closing price)
    - Explain why you think the stock changed, (review news and your own personal judgment)
    - Talk over the results with someone who is financially savvy

Some people forget that stock price changes can be explained by looking at the way in which the company does business or reviewing the news released that day.

Tracking Example

	Stock Symbol	Quantity Purchased	Price Purchased	Total Cost
Stock Info	APPL	5	$648.00	$3,280

Track Your Stock

	Date	Closing Price on Friday	Why do you think the stock changed?	Total Stock Value
Week 1	17 Aug	$648.00		$3,240.00
Week 2	24 Aug	$663.00		$3,315.00
Week 3	31 Aug	$665.00	.	$3,325.00
Week 4	7 Sept	$680.00		$3,400.00
Week 5	14 Sept	$691.00		$3,455.00
Week 6	21 Sept	$698.00	APPL—Apple released the new iPhone 5 on Thursday night.	$3,490.00
Week 7	28 Sept	$667.00	The new map application had malfunctions.	$3,335.00
Week 8	5 Oct	$652.00		$3,260.00

I purposely did not fill out all the *"Why do you think the stock changed."* Often, you invest in a stock because you see an opportunity to make money. This example tracks the movement of Apple (APPL) for 8 weeks.

1. I used this tracking sheet to predict why APPL's price would change.
   APPLE is releasing its new iPhone 5 in one month.
2. I then hypothesized how much it would go up.
   APPLE's price should rise by more than 5% or approximately $33.00.

Finally, I tracked whether my theory was right. I actually was both right and wrong in my prediction of Apple Stock.

1. I asked myself why I was right.
   Apple's stock rose as much as $50.00 because APPLE sold out of all iPhones.
2. I also asked myself why I was wrong,
   The stock also went down a week later due to the map application malfunctioning. If I had invested in this stock, I should have sold my five shares on week five or six, just in case.

Luckily this was a practice example. I didn't gain or lose any money. If I had invested approximately $3,300 in August, I would have made a $160.00 profit on around September 20. This is an example of tracking a stock and gauging how accurate your theory is on why the stock price changed.

Tracking Template - (For Practice)

Stock Info	Stock Symbol	Quantity Purchased	Price Purchased	Total Cost

Track Your Stock

	Date	Closing Price on Friday	Why do you think the stock changed?	Total Stock Value
Week 1				
Week 2				
Week 3				
Week 4				
Week 5				
Week 6				
Week 7				
Week 8				

"How can you become an artist if you never practice drawing? How can you become a great investor without practicing how to invest? Practice investing, not only to be a great investor, but that so you don't make mistakes like I did and lose $800 in 2 hours."

The Point:

"Don't lose money – Practice Investing"

Resources

- ☑ **Investment Account**
- ☑ **$1,500 - $3,000 in savings to start investing**
- ☑ *Websites to Practice Investing*
- ☐ Websites to Research Investing

Knowledge

- ☐ Do I understand generally how the stock market works?
- ☐ Do I know how to read a stock graph?
- ☐ Do I know the basics on how and why stock prices change?

Questions for Yourself

- ☑ **Am I investing with money that is not essential for my survival, such as rent, food, electricity, car payment?**
- ☐ Do I know whom to go to if I have any questions?
- ☐ Am I aware that I could lose money when I invest?
- ☐ Am I comfortable knowing that I may make mistakes when I invest and that these mistakes will show me what not to do and help build my experience as an investor?
- ☐ Do I know how to purchase and sell stocks through my investment account?

Critical Thinking

- ☐ Do I know how to predict whether or not a company will go bankrupt?
- ☐ Do I know how to research a company and make my own conclusions about whether or not I should invest?
- ☐ Do I know how to determine why a stock price will change (increase or decrease?)

Chap 4: *Research Companies*

Luckily,

We are not 6 years old

We may know where babies come from, but do we

KNOW OUR COMPANY?

To Know Our Company
We Must Understand
Risk Vs. Reward

Risk		Reward
"*Chance*" that you could "*Lose Money*" on your investment	VS	"Opportunity" you could "Earn a Profit" on your investment

More Risk = More Reward
Stock BETA: An Investors Best Friend

A Tool and a friend when evaluating Risk and Reward

Investopedia – Understanding BETA

This YouTube Video below is a must watch.

Created by Investopedia.com:
They explain the meaning of a BETA and
how it works for the Average Joe.

Tinyurl.com/StockBeta

Where can I find the BETA of a Stock?

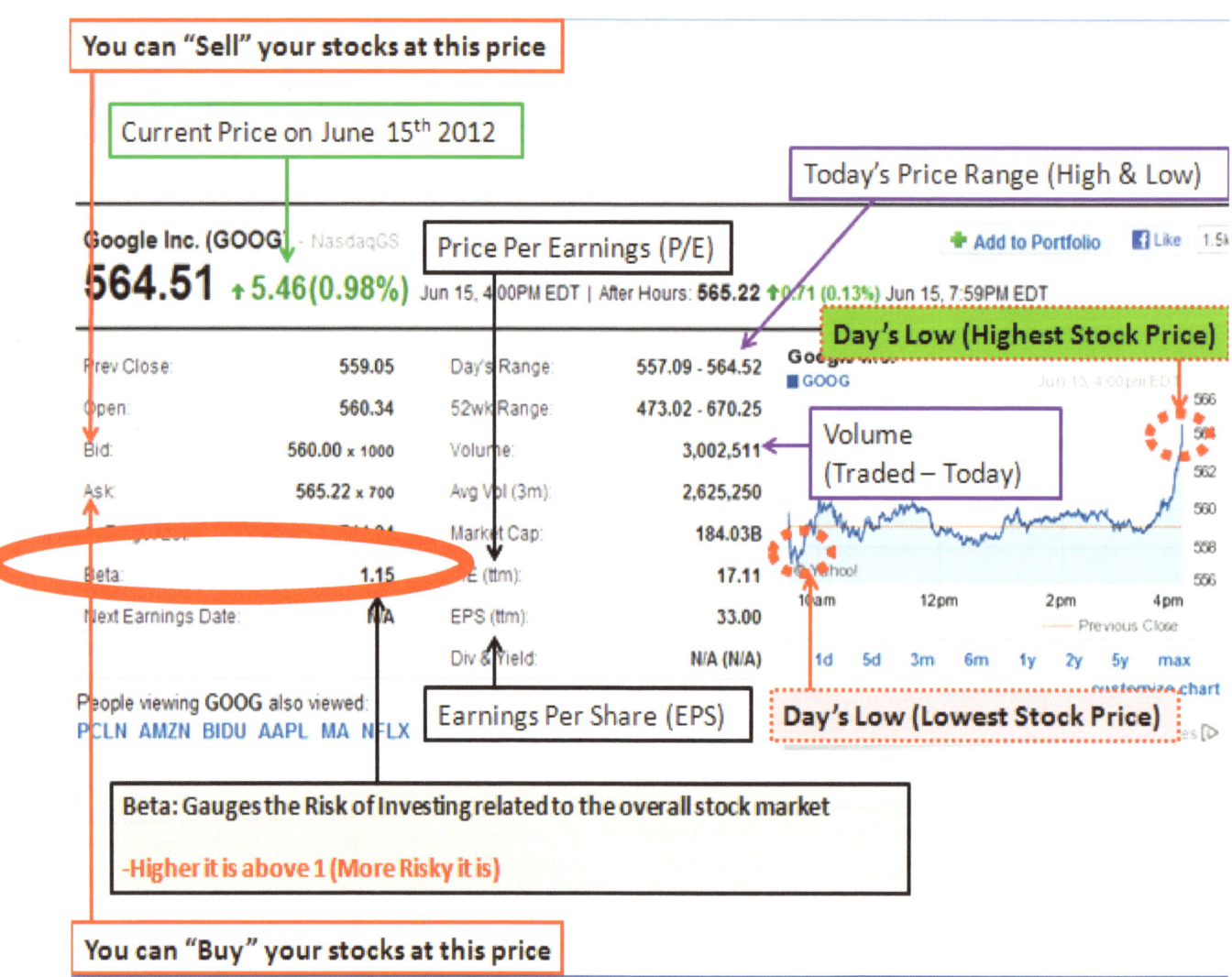

You can "Sell" your stocks at this price

Current Price on June 15th 2012

Today's Price Range (High & Low)

Price Per Earnings (P/E)

Day's Low (Highest Stock Price)

Volume (Traded – Today)

Earnings Per Share (EPS)

Day's Low (Lowest Stock Price)

Beta: Gauges the Risk of Investing related to the overall stock market

-Higher it is above 1 (More Risky it is)

You can "Buy" your stocks at this price

Resources to
KNOW YOUR COMPANY

Motley Fool – Stock Screener

This website has similar features to Yahoo except that actual investors write blogs and give direct opinions on specific stocks, ratings, etc. Motley Fool is reputable enough to make a rational prediction about stocks, using, of course, the insight of other resources as well.

www.caps.fool.com

Resources to
KNOW YOUR COMPANY

Yahoo Finance

Great for researching
Graphs
Prices of stocks
News updates on stocks
Beta rating of a stock

The higher the beta is from 1, the more risky it is than the stock market as a whole.

Personal Note: Get the I-Phone/Android App; it is very useful for finding the stocks that decreased and increased the most on a given day. (Use this feature to scout out opportunity.)

www.finance.yahoo.com

Resources to
KNOW YOUR COMPANY

Yahoo Finance – Stock Screener

The following Web link allows you to review stocks from various industries from health care to construction. It is an application that allows you to conduct an advanced search on stocks in a specific industry at a specific price.

Actual Link

http://screener.finance.yahoo.com/stocks.html

Shortened Link

Tinyurl.com/YahooStockScouter

Resources to
KNOW YOUR COMPANY

MSN Money – Stock Scouter

This website gives you the rating and the pros and cons of each stock.

It is an amazing resource for quick research.

(Feel free to type in "MSN Money – Stock Scouter" on Google to find this as well.)

Actual Link

Money.msn.com/investing/stockscouter-stock-ratings.aspx

Shortened Link

Tinyurl.com/MsnStockScouter

Resources to
KNOW YOUR COMPANY

Help Island Stock Rating System

This is a great website. It compares how many people are buying stock compared to selling stock. This site can be a measure for you to evaluate whether one should buy or not. However, I would advise reviewing other websites for more opinions. Because this website contains complicated terminology, it is definitely for the more advanced investor.

Link

Stock.Helpisland.com

To create a masterpiece you need to know your masterpiece. To invest, you must KNOW your company, and know what it does and why the stocks change

The Point:

"Research – Know Your Company"

Congratulations!! You are just a little bit closer to becoming an investor.

The Points that are **Bolded in RED** are the points we have covered in this chapter!

Before you move on to the next chapter, you should understand why these concepts are essential in order for you to become an investor. Keep on reading! You are doing great!

Resources

☑ **Investment Account**

☑ **$1,500 - $3,000 in savings to start investing**

☑ **Websites to Practice Investing**

☑ *Websites to Research Investing*

Knowledge

☐ Do I understand generally how the stock market works?

☐ Do I know how to read a stock graph?

☐ Do I know the basics on how and why stock prices change?

Questions for Yourself

☑ **Am I investing with money that is not essential for my survival, such as rent, food, electricity, car payment?**

☐ Do I know whom to go to if I have any questions?

☐ Am I aware that I could lose money when I invest?

☐ Am I comfortable knowing that I may make mistakes when I invest and that these mistakes will show me what not to do and help build my experience as an investor?

☐ Do I know how to purchase and sell stocks through my investment account?

Critical Thinking

☐ Do I know how to predict whether or not a company will go bankrupt?

☐ Do I know how to research a company and make my own conclusions about whether or not I should invest?

☐ Do I know how to determine why a stock price will change (increase or decrease?)

Chap 5: *Understand Investing*

When you take your driving test for the first time, you are not an expert, but you know how to drive.

The same is true with investing; you don't have to be an expert to know how to invest, but you must at least *UNDERSTAND* how to invest.

Understand Investing

You don't need to be an expert.

But you should understand the basics.

Companies may care about the performance of their stock because

- Companies can receive a *bigger credit limit.*
- Shareholders (people who own stock) can vote to *fire the managers* of the company.
- They don't want their company to be *taken over* due to low stock price.
- *CEO's own stock* and want the stock prices to go up so they make more money

Concept:

Why are companies in the stock market?

Key Point:

Companies go on the stock market because they can receive money from their (IPO)—initial public offering.

They usually use this money to grow their company.

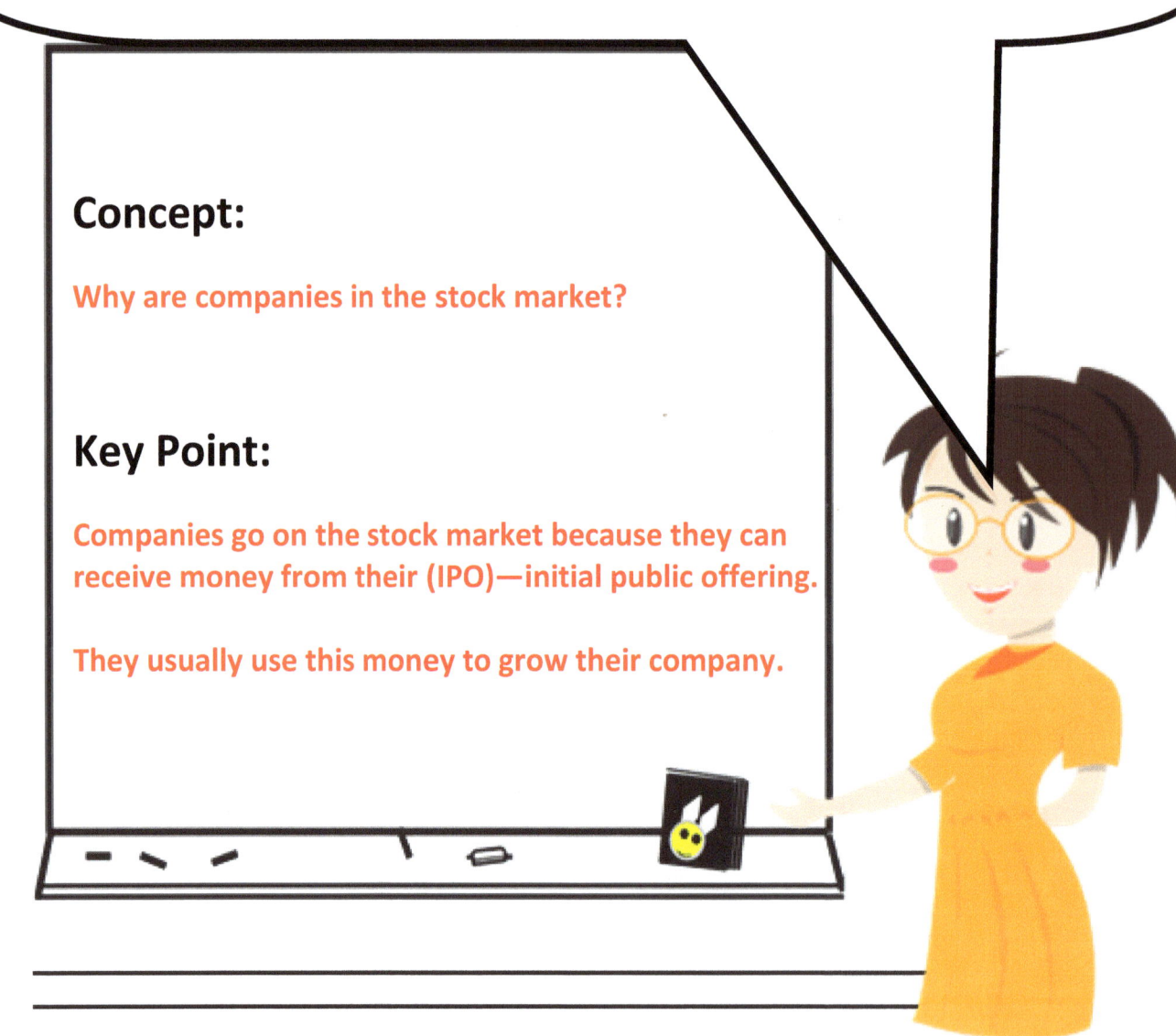

Concept: What does it mean to own a stock?

Key Points:

How much are you willing to pay to
own a part of my company?

When you own a share or stock, you own
A % (a part or percentage) of a company.

The more shares or stocks you own,
the more money you _gain_ when the price goes up.

The more shares or stocks you own,
the more money you _lose_ when the price goes down.

The price of a stock is determined by the people who own shares of the company.

What is the world willing to pay to own a part of the company?

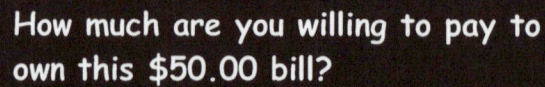

Stock Analogy

When you buy a stock, you are hoping that people will pay more for it in the future.

Example:

One stock of Apple is worth $500 today.

The iPhone 5 releases in 2 weeks.
You think the stock price will go up to $550.00 (10%).

Why? You think that Apple will earn more money because it will sell a lot of iPhones in the next month.
Thus, people will pay more to own stocks of Apple because more people are buying the stock.

Basically, the stock price is determined by two things.

1. How much are people willing to pay for a stock?
2. How many people are trying to buy the stock?

Think of it this way…

- People will pay hundreds of dollars for old baseball cards. Why? There are more people trying to buy these baseball cards than there are baseball cards.

The more people there are trying to buy something, the more it will cost.

The same goes for stocks. If a company is doing well, people will pay more money for stocks because they think the stocks will continue to increase.

Let's Read a Graph!

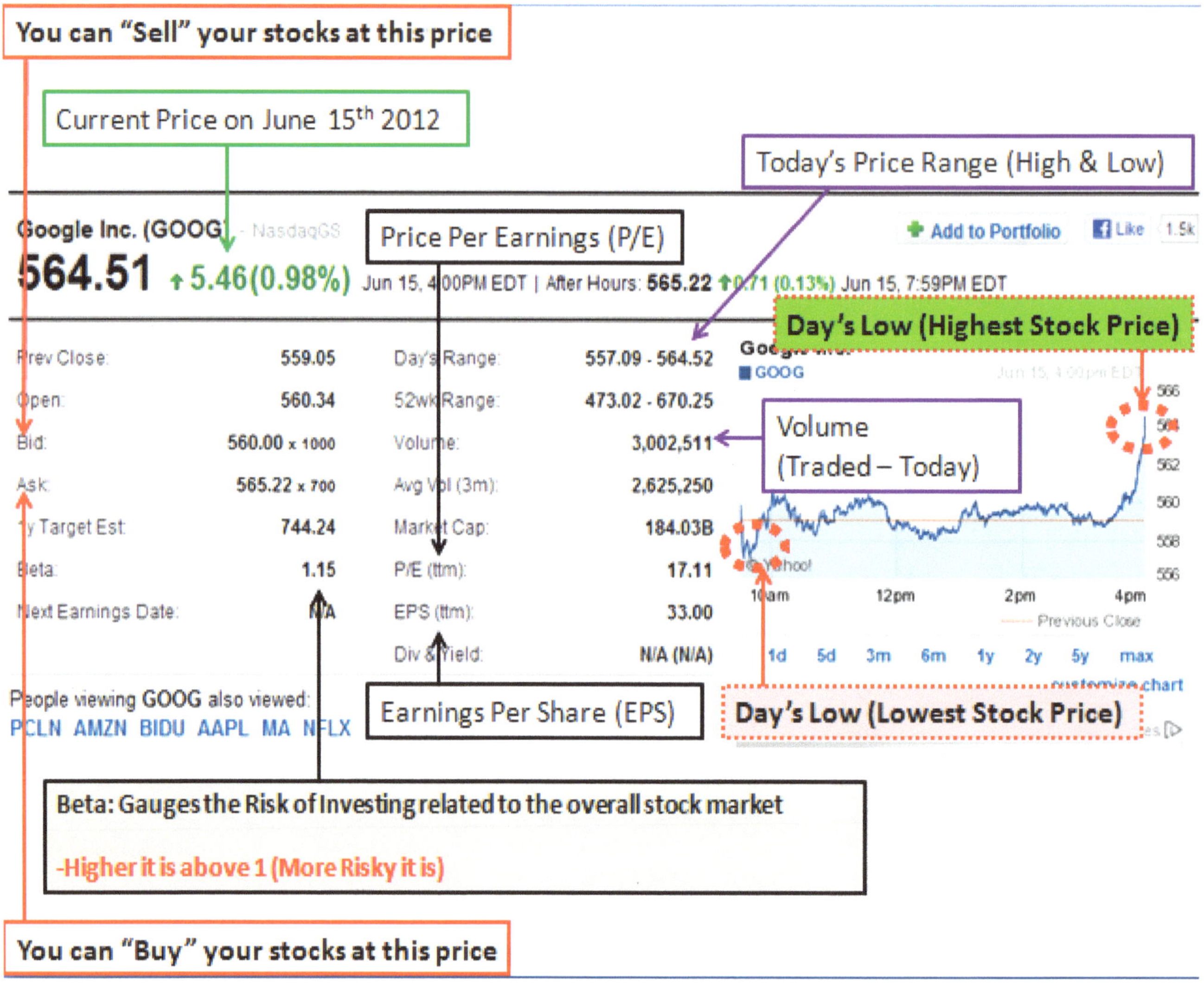

You can "Sell" your stocks at this price

Current Price on June 15th 2012

Today's Price Range (High & Low)

Price Per Earnings (P/E)

Google Inc. (GOOG) - NasdaqGS

564.51 ↑ 5.46(0.98%) Jun 15, 4:00PM EDT | After Hours: **565.22** ↑0.71 (0.13%) Jun 15, 7:59PM EDT

Day's Low (Highest Stock Price)

Prev Close:	559.05	Day's Range:	557.09 - 564.52
Open:	560.34	52wk Range:	473.02 - 670.25
Bid:	560.00 x 1000	Volume:	3,002,511
Ask:	565.22 x 700	Avg Vol (3m):	2,625,250
1y Target Est:	744.24	Market Cap:	184.03B
Beta:	1.15	P/E (ttm):	17.11
Next Earnings Date:	N/A	EPS (ttm):	33.00
		Div & Yield:	N/A (N/A)

Volume (Traded – Today)

GOOG
■ GOOG   Jun 15, 4:00pm EDT
566
564
562
560
558
556
10am   12pm   2pm   4pm
— Previous Close
1d 5d 3m 6m 1y 2y 5y max
customize chart

People viewing GOOG also viewed:
PCLN AMZN BIDU AAPL MA NFLX

Earnings Per Share (EPS)

Day's Low (Lowest Stock Price)

Beta: Gauges the Risk of Investing related to the overall stock market

-Higher it is above 1 (More Risky it is)

You can "Buy" your stocks at this price

Why did the Stock Change?

Tsunami vs. Tokyo Power Plant

Tsunami in Japan → realized stock price will drop

1. I waited for the stock price to drop and for the stock to bottom out.
2. I did research and realized that at that time nuclear energy made up over 20% of Japan's energy.
3. I predicted that it was too big to fail in the short term (next three months).
4. I bought a few hundred stocks at a very low price.
5. I sold the stocks and made money.

Why Did the Stock Change?

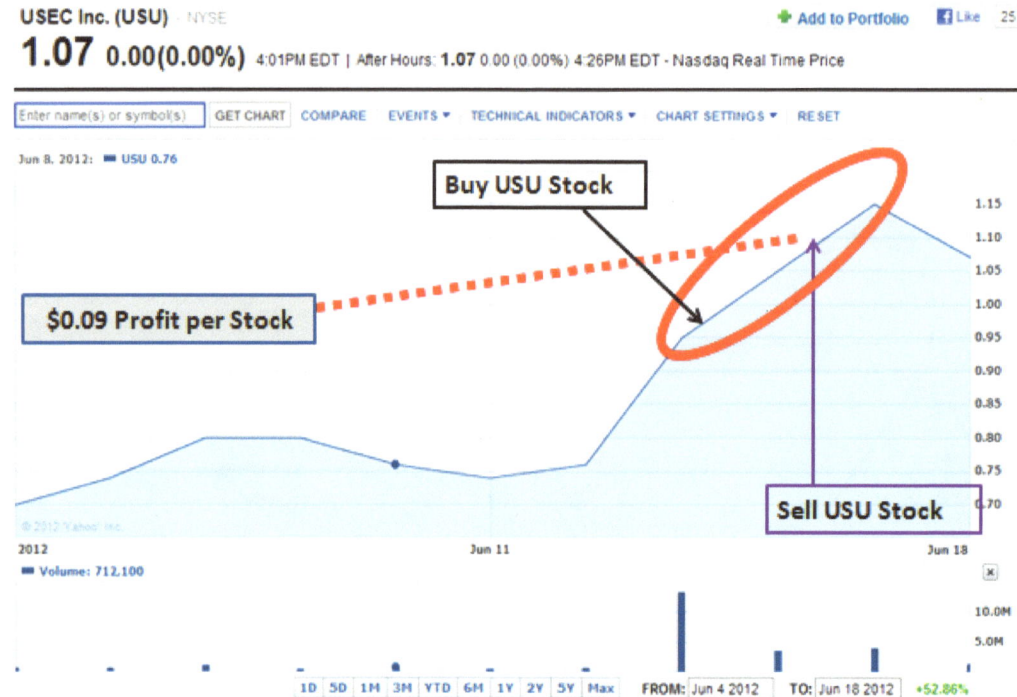

Government Loan Causes Hype

USEC Inc. (USU) NYSE   + Add to Portfolio   Like 25

1.07 0.00(0.00%) 4:01PM EDT | After Hours: **1.07** 0.00 (0.00%) 4:26PM EDT - Nasdaq Real Time Price

Enter name(s) or symbol(s)   GET CHART   COMPARE   EVENTS ▾   TECHNICAL INDICATORS ▾   CHART SETTINGS ▾   RESET

Jun 8, 2012 : ▬ USU 0.76

Buy USU Stock

$0.09 Profit per Stock

Sell USU Stock

2012   Jun 11   Jun 18

▬ Volume: 712,100

© 2012 Yahoo! Inc.

1D 5D 1M 3M YTD 6M 1Y 2Y 5Y Max   FROM: Jun 4 2012   TO: Jun 18 2012   +52.86%

Government loan → Realized stock price will go up due to good news

1. I predicted USU would go up by $0.10 or so due to good news and to investors buying shares because of the news of the U.S. loan.
2. I predicted USU was not going bankrupt in the next six months and that uranium demand would go up in the next six months due to demand from China and India.
3. I bought 1,000 shares.
4. I sold the stocks within a few days and made money.

Why did the Stock Change?

Skullcandy Headphones will Rebound

Skullcandy, Inc. (SKUL) - NasdaqGS

13.25 ↓0.35(2.57%) 3:40PM EDT - Nasdaq Real Time Price

Add to Portfolio   Like   19

Enter name(s) or symbol(s) | GET CHART   COMPARE   EVENTS ▼   TECHNICAL INDICATORS ▼   CHART SETTINGS ▼   RESET

Sep 28, 2012: ■ SKUL 13.75

SKUL Drops because of JP Morgan's Comments

I purchased 100 Shares Here at $12.80

I sold the shares here at $13.75

Volume: 484,400

1D 5D 1M 3M 6M YTD 1Y 2Y   FROM: Sep 10 2012 TO: Oct 10 2012   -10.92%

SKUL stock price would go up in the short term.

1. I realized JP Morgan had made statements that caused the stock price to decrease by over 15% but the statements it made were only true in the long term not the short term.
2. I predicted the stock price would rebound the next day.
3. The stock price rebounded by about 9% the next day.
4. I sold the stocks within three weeks and made money.

Why did the Stock Change?

BP – Too big to fail

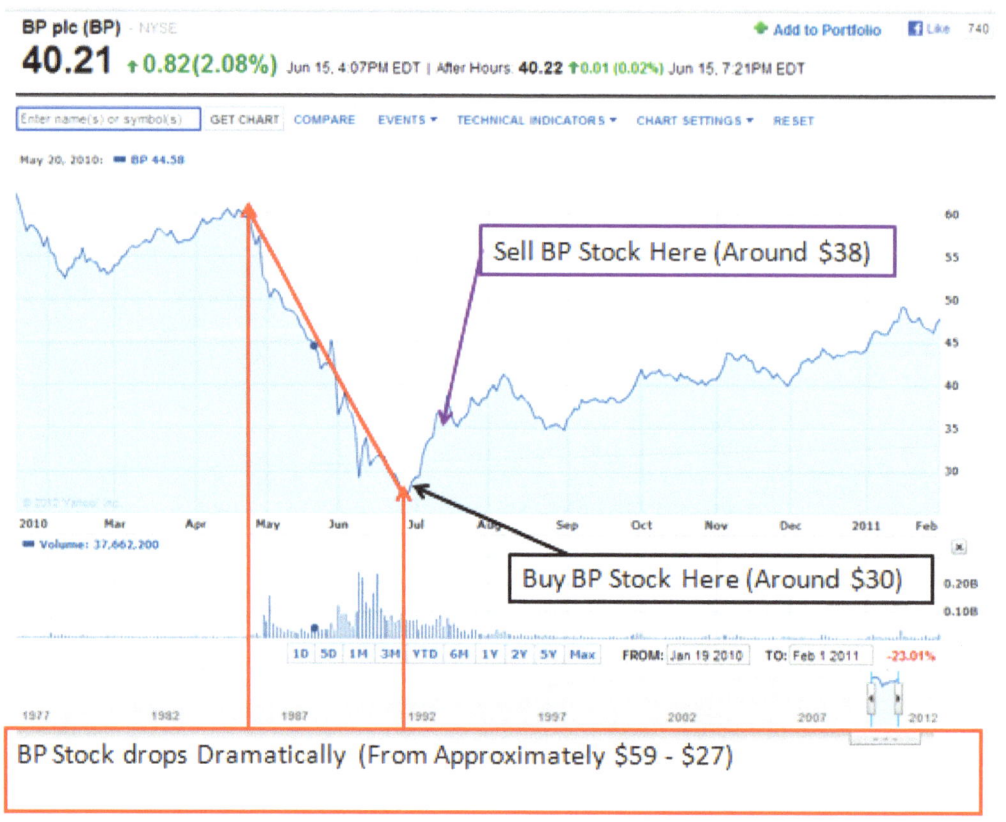

BP Stock drops Dramatically (From Approximately $59 - $27)

BP stock price would rebound within six months.

1. BP's stock price dropped by $30.
2. You would have realized that BP was too big to fail and that the U.S. government could not take it down.
3. You would have bought the stock at its low.
4. You would have sold the stock when it jumped about $7 or so.

Why did the Stock Change?

Event Investing Examples

Look for these types of events below. In many cases, when these events occur, it gives investors an opportunity to make some money.

- Natural disaster
- Political favoritism toward industry
- Political bailout
- Global recession
- Companies merging (two companies becoming one company)
- Potentially securing a deal in an industry
- Company potentially reducing debt
- Opportunity for growth
- Company found ways to cut costs
- Seasonal industry—prices rise and fall
- Black October—seasonally, in October, many stocks naturally fall.
- Buy low—sell high

Because the stock market is not perfect, the market can oversell good or bad news, and in turn, you make money.

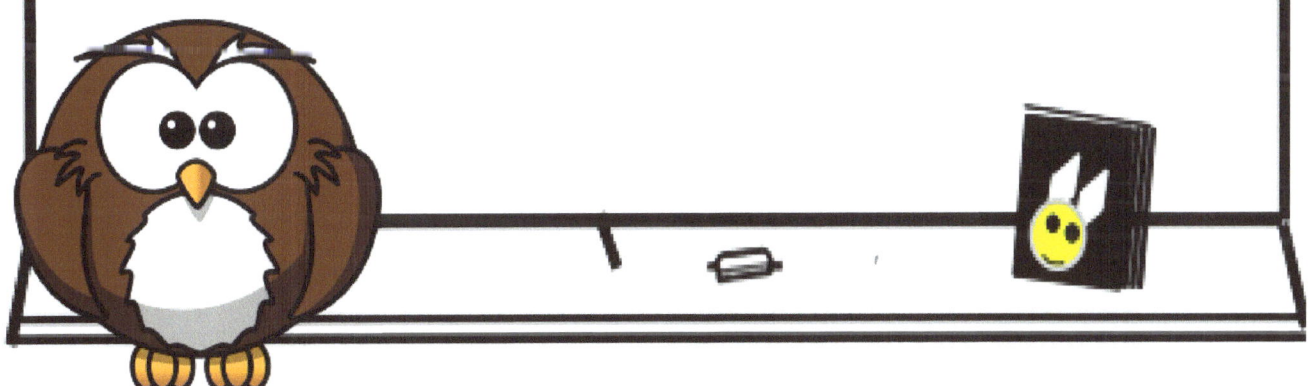

"You may not be an expert when you start your career as an artist, but you understand how to draw, you comprehend what colors to use, and you recognize you will need to learn more to become an expert artist."

The Point:
      Understand Basic Investing
        Then Learn More…

Congratulations!! You are just a little bit closer to becoming an investor.

The Points that are Bolded in RED are the points we have covered in this chapter!

Before you move on to the next chapter, you should understand why these concepts are essential in order for you to become an investor. Keep on reading! You are doing great!

Resources

- ☑ **Investment Account**
- ☑ **$1,500 - $3,000 in savings to start investing**
- ☑ **Websites to Practice Investing**
- ☑ **Websites to Research Investing**

Knowledge

- ☑ *Do I understand generally how the stock market works?*
- ☑ *Do I know how to read a stock graph?*
- ☑ *Do I know the basics on how and why stock prices change?*

Questions for Yourself

- ☑ **Am I investing with money that is not essential for my survival, such as rent, food, electricity, car payment?**
- ☐ Do I know whom to go to if I have any questions?
- ☐ Am I aware that I could lose money when I invest?
- ☐ Am I comfortable knowing that I may make mistakes when I invest and that these mistakes will show me what not to do and help build my experience as an investor?
- ☐ Do I know how to purchase and sell stocks through my investment account?

Critical Thinking

- ☐ Do I know how to predict whether or not a company will go bankrupt?
- ☐ Do I know how to research a company and make my own conclusions about whether or not I should invest?
- ☐ Do I know how to determine why a stock price will change (increase or decrease?)

Chap 6: *Go Out and Do It*

Go Out and Do It!
Start Investing!

This purpose of this book was to give you a point and a place to go. You need to now GO! If you need help, here are some...

Resources to Learn More Information about Investing

Real Life and College Resources

- Newspaper
- Basic Finance Class
- Business Orientated Student Organizations
- Finance Professor
- Find an adult who invests and ask him/her to mentor you
- A friend that invests

The Internet

- Google
- Fool.com
- Investopedia.com
- Morningstar.com/cover/classroom.html
- A Basic Facebook Post asking an investment question
- Finance.yahoo.com

STOP!! Before you invest! Make sure you can check each tasks below.

The Tasks in RED Highlight what we have covered. The Tasks in Blue highlight what you will need to still learn how to do following reading this book.

Do not start investing real money until you can check off YES to all of below. If you can't, check yes to 100% of the questions, there is a very, very good chance you will lose money if you start.

Resources

 Investment Account

 $1,500 - $3,000 in savings to start investing

 Websites to Practice Investing

 Websites to Research Investing

Knowledge

 Do I understand generally how the stock market works?

 Do I know how to read a stock graph?

 Do I know the basics on how and why stock prices change?

Questions for Yourself

☑ Am I investing with money that is not essential for my survival, such as rent, food, electricity, car payment?

☑ Do I know whom to go to if I have any questions?

☐ Am I aware that I could lose money when I invest?

☐ Am I comfortable knowing that I may make mistakes when I invest and that these mistakes will show me what not to do and help build my experience as an investor?

☐ Do I know how to purchase and sell stocks through my investment account?

Critical Thinking

☐ Do I know how to predict whether or not a company will go bankrupt?

☐ Do I know how to research a company and make my own conclusions about whether or not I should invest?

☐ Do I know how to determine why a stock price will change (increase or decrease?)

Conclusion!

You don't know how it is to be an artist, until you draw something and sell it

You really don't know about relationships until you have one

You especially don't know about living on your own, until you have to

The Point:

"Investing is the same way:
The only way to know how to invest
is to take a chance and do it."

Project Ice Investing

My book, *Investing: Blunt and to the Point*, and my website, IceInvesting.com, are projects developed by Launch, LLC. IceInvesting.com is a free resource that goes hand-in-hand with my book. On this website, we consolidate some of the best video resources for intermediate investing. This website will help you further your knowledge of investing. (To be released March 2013)

www.IceInvesting.com

Our Partner Projects

Motivational Videos for Success

YouTube.com/LaunchMySuccess

A.I. Textbooks, LLC
Find the best price online for Textbooks

Awesome Ideas

AwesomeTextbooks.com

Copyright, Legal Notice and Disclaimer:

Finally, please be smart, be rational, please. Nothing in this book is designed to replace common sense, rationality, professional opinions, suggestions, advice, etc. This book is intended to be an enjoyable read, to give you some insight on a how a student invests with a small investment account.

As for sharing this document; I spent a lot of time putting this together; and I would really appreciate it, if it was not shared with individuals who had not paid for my eBook. It's not being greedy; it's just that if you put in the time and effort to write a book that is out there to help countless people; you wouldn't like if someone was pirating your book. Please don't do that. If the information in this book was helpful, then recommend it to a friend to purchase. It is not expensive for the amount of knowledge they may receive. Not to mention, you really cannot put a price on knowledge.

Lastly, it goes without saying that you can't post this document or information in it on websites, ftp sites, forums, etc.; I think you get my blunt rational. The place you can get my book will be (Web Site). Thanks for reading, and I really appreciate your support for my first book.

Thanks :) :)

Joshua B. Anton